Essential Insights from the spiri
of Bahá'u'lláh, 'Abdu'l-Bahá and

Awareness

Compiled and designed by Corinne Randall

To Masoud Yazdani, whose vision inspired the creation of these books,
you will always be in our hearts.

Purpose

The All-loving God created man
to radiate the Divine Light,
and to illuminate the world
by his words, action, and life.

Man has been created for
the knowledge and love of God,
for the virtues of the human world,
for spirituality, heavenly
illumination and eternal life.

Ye are the stars of the heaven of understanding, the breeze that stirreth at the break of day, the soft-flowing waters upon which must depend the very life of all men, the letters inscribed upon His sacred scroll.

'Abdu'l-Bahá

Having created the world and all that liveth and moveth therein, He, through the direct operation of His unconstrained and sovereign Will, chose to confer upon man the unique distinction and capacity to know Him and to love Him—a capacity that must needs be regarded as the generating impulse and the primary purpose underlying the whole of creation….

Upon the inmost reality of each and every created thing He hath shed the light of one of His names, and made it a recipient of the glory of one of His attributes. Upon the reality of man, however, He hath focused the radiance of all of His names and attributes, and made it a mirror of His own Self. Alone of all created things man hath been singled out for so great a favour, so enduring a bounty.

Bahá'u'lláh

Education

These energies with which the Day Star of Divine bounty and Source of heavenly guidance hath endowed the reality of man lie, however, latent within him, even as the flame is hidden within the candle and the rays of light are potentially present in the lamp. The radiance of these energies may be obscured by worldly desires even as the light of the sun can be concealed beneath the dust and dross which cover the mirror. Neither the candle nor the lamp can be lighted through their own unaided efforts, nor can it ever be possible for the mirror to free itself from its dross…

Until a fire is kindled the lamp will never be ignited, and unless the dross is blotted out from the face of the mirror it can never represent the image of the sun nor reflect its light and glory... Then, and only then, will the Trust of God, latent in the reality of man, emerge, as resplendent as the rising Orb of Divine Revelation, from behind the veil of concealment, and implant the ensign of its revealed glory upon the summits of men's hearts.

Bahá'u'lláh

And since there can be no tie of direct intercourse to bind the one true God with His creation, and no resemblance whatever can exist between the transient and the Eternal, the contingent and the Absolute, He hath ordained that in every age and dispensation a pure and stainless Soul be made manifest in the kingdoms of earth and heaven.… These resplendent Realities are the channels of God's all-pervasive grace. Led by the light of unfailing guidance, and invested with supreme sovereignty, They are commissioned to use the inspiration of Their words, the effusions of Their infallible grace and the sanctifying breeze of Their Revelation for the cleansing of every longing heart and receptive spirit from the dross and dust of earthly cares and limitations.

Bahá'u'lláh

Man is the supreme Talisman. Lack of a proper education hath, however, deprived him of that which he doth inherently possess. Through a word proceeding out of the mouth of God he was called into being; by one word more he was guided to recognize the Source of his education; by yet another word his station and destiny were safeguarded.

The Great Being saith: Regard man as a mine rich in gems of inestimable value. Education can, alone, cause it to reveal its treasures, and enable mankind to benefit therefrom.

Bahá'u'lláh

Unknowable Essence

How can I claim to have known Thee, when the entire creation is bewildered by Thy mystery, and how can I confess not to have known Thee, when, lo, the whole universe proclaimeth Thy Presence and testifieth to Thy truth?

All else besides Him have been created by His behest, have been fashioned by His leave, are subject to His law, are as a thing forgotten when compared to the glorious evidences of His oneness, and are as nothing when brought face to face with the mighty revelations of His unity.

Bahá'u'lláh

The birds of men's hearts, however high they soar, can never hope to attain the heights of His unknowable Essence. Far be it from His glory that human pen or tongue should hint at His mystery, or that human heart conceive His Essence. All else besides Him stand poor and desolate at His door, all are powerless before the greatness of His might, all are but slaves in His Kingdom.

The tie of servitude established between the worshipper and the adored One, between the creature and the Creator, should in itself be regarded as a token of His gracious favour unto men, and not as an indication of any merit they may possess. To this testifieth every true and discerning believer.

Bahá'u'lláh

Word of God

The Word of God—exalted be His glory—is higher and far superior to that which the senses can perceive, for it is sanctified from any property or substance. It transcendeth the limitations of known elements and is exalted above all the essential and recognized substances. It became manifest without any syllable or sound and is none but the Command of God which pervadeth all created things. It hath never been withheld from the world of being. It is God's all-pervasive grace, from which all grace doth emanate. It is an entity far removed above all that hath been and shall be.

Behold how, in this Day, the Beginning
is reflected in the End,
how out of Stillness
motion hath been engendered.
This motion hath been generated
by the potent energies
which the words of the Almighty
have released throughout the entire creation.

Bahá'u'lláh

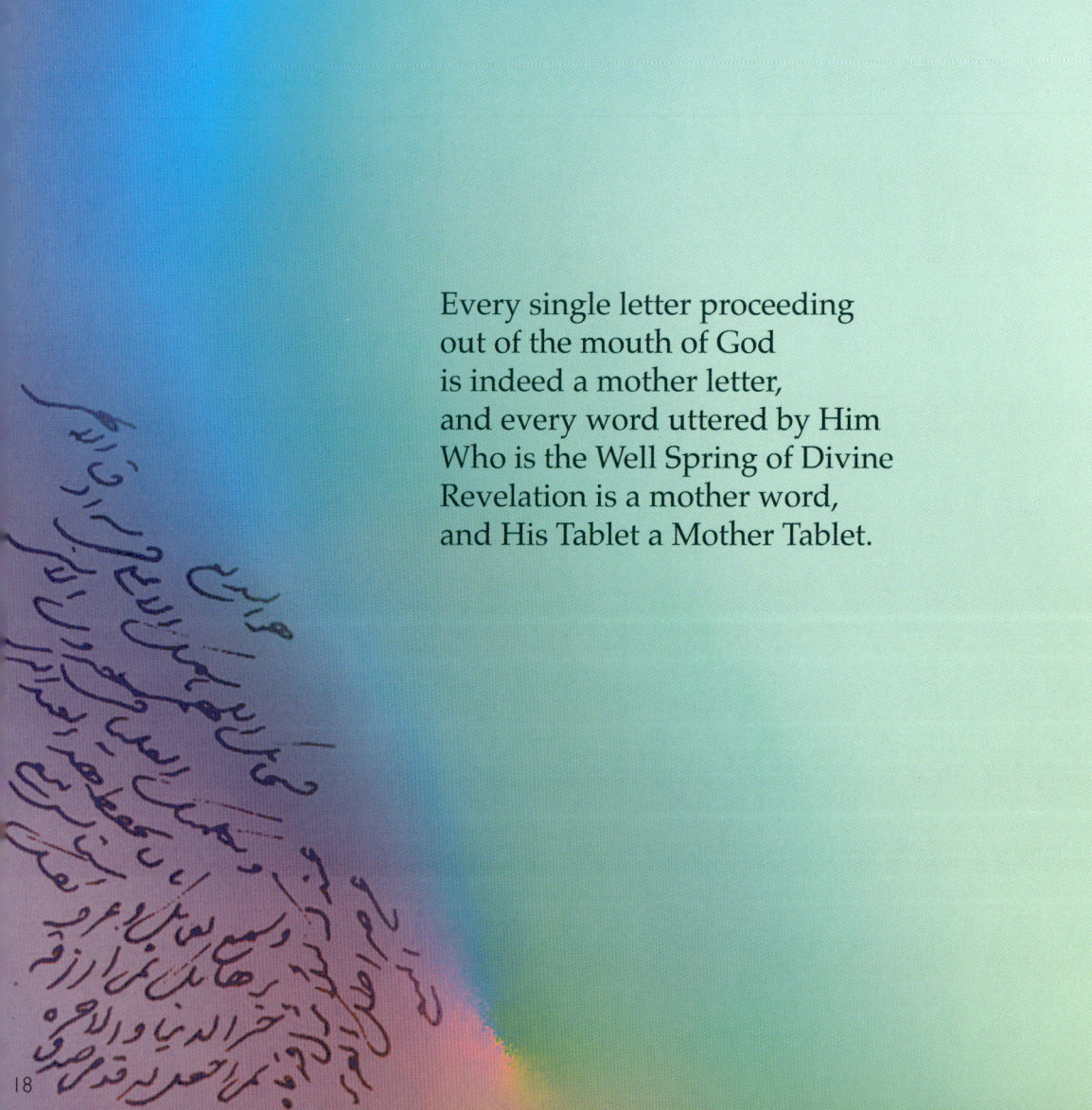

Every single letter proceeding
out of the mouth of God
is indeed a mother letter,
and every word uttered by Him
Who is the Well Spring of Divine
Revelation is a mother word,
and His Tablet a Mother Tablet.

All the wondrous works ye behold in this world have been manifested through the operation of His supreme and most exalted Will, His wondrous and inflexible Purpose. Through the mere revelation of the word "Fashioner," issuing forth from His lips and proclaiming His attribute to mankind, such power is released as can generate, through successive ages, all the manifold arts which the hands of man can produce.

Bahá'u'lláh

Consultation

The Great Being saith: The heaven of divine wisdom is illumined with the two luminaries of consultation and compassion. Take ye counsel together in all matters, inasmuch as consultation is the lamp of guidance which leadeth the way, and is the bestower of understanding.

Consultation bestows greater awareness and transmutes conjecture into certitude. It is a shining light which, in a dark world, leads the way and guides. For everything there is and will continue to be a station of perfection and maturity. The maturity of the gift of understanding is made manifest through consultation.

Bahá'u'lláh

The eternal soul

The mind comprehendeth the abstract by the aid of the concrete, but the soul hath limitless manifestations of its own. The mind is circumscribed, the soul limitless…It is by the aid of such senses as those of sight, hearing, taste, smell and touch, that the mind comprehendeth, whereas the soul is free from all agencies.

The soul…whether it be in sleep or waking,
is in motion and ever active.
Possibly it may, whilst in a dream,
unravel an intricate problem,
incapable of solution in the waking state.

'Abdu'l-Bahá

"Two wings" of the soul

One is the wing of knowledge, the other of faith.
This is the means of the ascent of the human soul
to the lofty station of divine perfections.

'Abdu'l-Bahá

The human soul is exalted above all egress and regress. It is still, and yet it soareth; it moveth, and yet it is still. It is, in itself, a testimony that beareth witness to the existence of a world that is contingent, as well as to the reality of a world that hath neither beginning nor end.

Bahá'u'lláh

The Kingdom is the world of vision where all the
concealed realities will become disclosed….
The mysteries of which man is heedless in this earthly
world, those he will discover in the heavenly world,
and there will he be informed of the secret of truth.

'Abdu'l-Bahá

That divine world is manifestly a world of lights; therefore man has need of illumination here. That is a world of love; the love of God is essential. It is a world of perfections; virtues or perfections must be acquired. That world is vivified by the breaths of the Holy Spirit; in this world we must seek them. That is the Kingdom of life everlasting; it must be attained during this vanishing existence.

It is similar to the condition of a human being in the womb, where his eyes are veiled, and all things are hidden away from him. Once he is born out of the uterine world and entereth this life, he findeth it, with relation to that of the womb, to be a place of perceptions and discoveries, and he observeth all things through his outer eye. In the same way, once he hath departed this life, he will behold, in that world whatsoever was hidden from him here: but there he will look upon and comprehend all things with his inner eye.

'Abdu'l-Bahá

Insight

The more we search for ourselves,
the less likely we are to find ourselves;
and the more we search for God,
and to serve our fellow-men,
the more profoundly will we become
acquainted with ourselves,
and the more inwardly assured.

Shoghi Effendi

Frequently doth man become forgetful of his own self, whilst God remaineth, through His all-encompassing knowledge, aware of His creature, and continueth to shed upon him the manifest radiance of His glory. It is evident, therefore, that, in such circumstances, He is closer to him than his own self.

Bahá'u'lláh

Look at the world and ponder a while upon it. It unveileth the book of its own self before thine eyes and revealeth that which the Pen of thy Lord, the Fashioner, the All-Informed, hath inscribed therein.

Nature is God's Will and is its expression in and through the contingent world…Indeed a man of insight can perceive naught therein save the effulgent splendour of Our Name, the Creator. Say: This is an existence which knoweth no decay, and Nature itself is lost in bewilderment before its revelations, its compelling evidences and its effulgent glory which have encompassed the universe.

Bahá'u'lláh

When… thou dost contemplate the innermost essence of all things, and the individuality of each, thou wilt behold the signs of thy Lord's mercy in every created thing, and see the spreading rays of His Names and Attributes throughout all the realm of being.

Then wilt thou observe that the universe is a scroll that discloseth His hidden secrets, which are preserved in the well-guarded Tablet. And not an atom of all the atoms in existence, not a creature from amongst the creatures but speaketh His praise and telleth of His attributes and names, revealeth the glory of His might and guideth to His oneness and His mercy.

'Abdu'l-Bahá

The more pure and sanctified the heart of man becomes, the nearer it draws to God, and the light of the Sun of Reality is revealed within it.

This light sets hearts aglow with the fire of the love of God, opens in them the doors of knowledge and unseals the divine mysteries so that spiritual discoveries are made possible.

'Abdu'l-Bahá

O Lord, help Thou Thy loved ones to acquire knowledge and the sciences and arts, and to unravel the secrets that are treasured up in the inmost reality of all created beings. Make them to hear the hidden truths that are written and embedded in the heart of all that is.

'Abdu'l-Bahá

Behold the most subtle realities of His dominion... fathom the mysteries of His kingdom... perceive the signs of His transcendent Essence in this mortal world... attain a station wherein one seeth no distinction amongst His creatures and findeth no flaw in the creation of the heavens and the earth.

Bahá'u'lláh

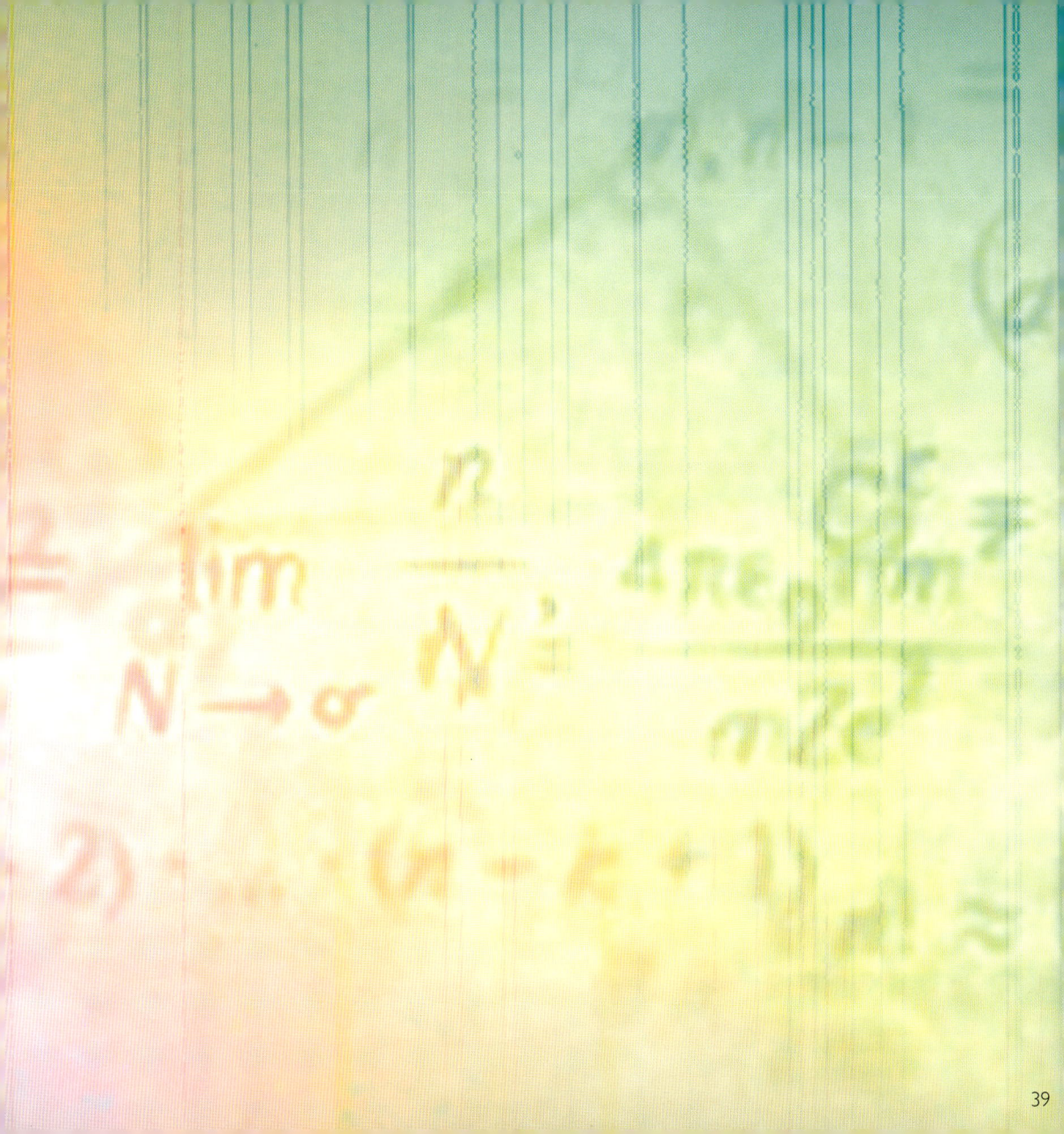

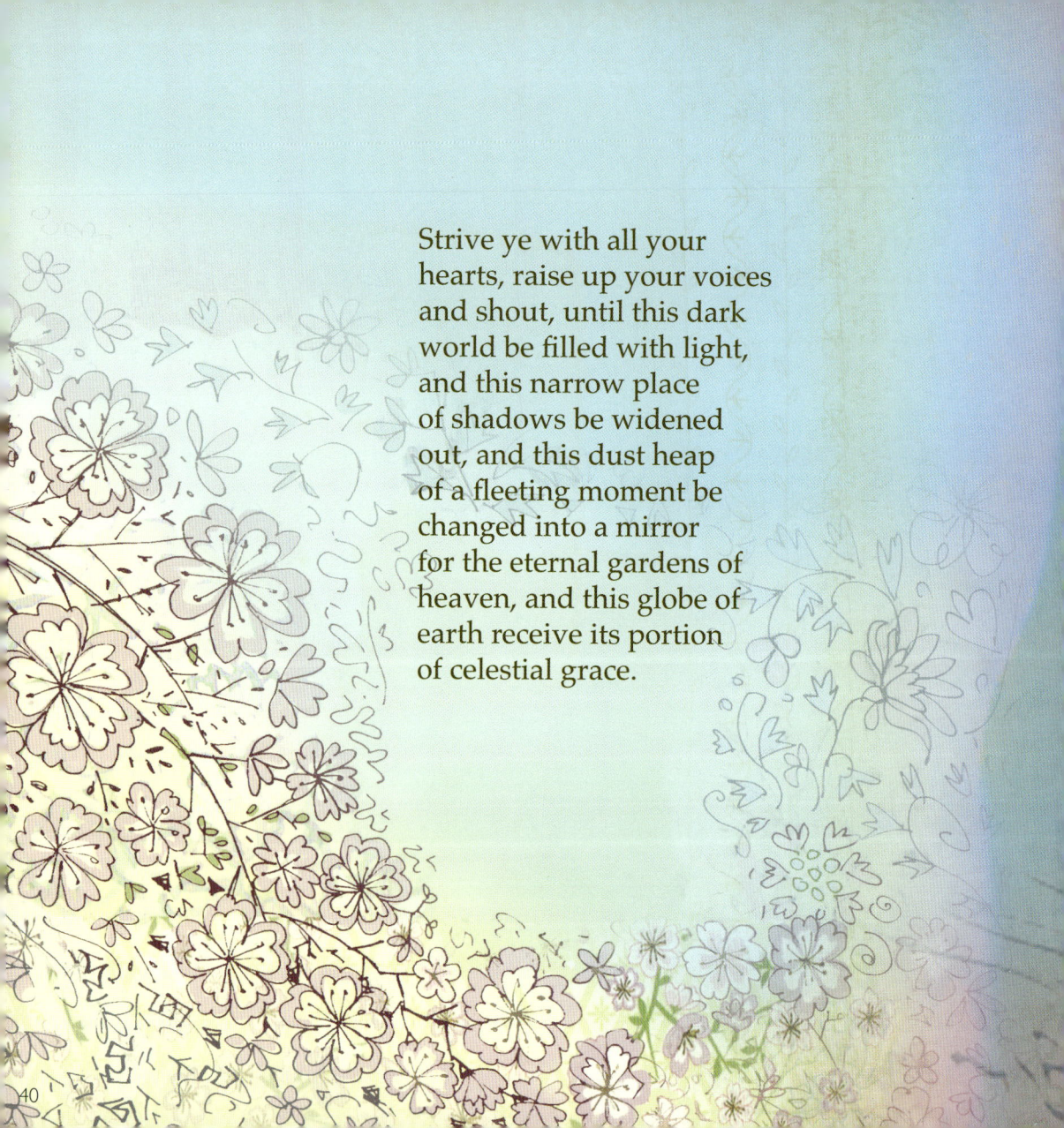

Strive ye with all your hearts, raise up your voices and shout, until this dark world be filled with light, and this narrow place of shadows be widened out, and this dust heap of a fleeting moment be changed into a mirror for the eternal gardens of heaven, and this globe of earth receive its portion of celestial grace.

The portals of His blessings are opened wide and His signs are published abroad and the glory of truth is blazing forth; inexhaustible are the blessings.

'Abdu'l-Bahá

O MY FRIENDS!

Have ye forgotten that true and radiant morn, when in those hallowed and blessed surroundings ye were all gathered in My presence beneath the shade of the tree of life, which is planted in the all-glorious paradise? Awe-struck ye listened as I gave utterance to these three most holy words:

O friends! Prefer not your will to Mine, never desire that which I have not desired for you, and approach Me not with lifeless hearts, defiled with worldly desires and cravings.

Would ye but sanctify your souls, ye would at this present hour recall that place and those surroundings, and the truth of My utterance should be made evident unto all of you.

Bahá'u'lláh

At the time when We were hidden behind countless veils of light thou didst commune with Me and didst witness the luminaries of the heaven of My wisdom and the billows of the ocean of Mine utterance. Verily thy Lord is the Truthful, the Faithful. Great indeed is the blessedness of him who hath attained the liberal effusions of this ocean in the days of his Lord, the Most Bountiful, the All-Wise.

Bahá'u'lláh

REFERENCES

p. 2a	'Abdu'l-Bahá, *Paris Talks*, UK Bahá'í Publishing Trust, 1972, p.113
p. 2b	'Abdu'l-Bahá, *The Promulgation of Universal Peace*, US Bahá'í Publishing Trust, 1982, p.226
p. 3.	Bahá'u'lláh, *Gleanings from the Writings of Bahá'u'lláh*, US Bahá'i Publishing Trust, 1990 pocket-size edition, XCVI: p.196
pp. 4-5.	*ibid*, XXVII: p.65
pp. 6-7.	*ibid*, pp.65-6
p. 8.	*ibid*, pp.66-7
p. 10-11.	Bahá'u'lláh, *Gleanings from the Writings of Bahá'u'lláh*, US Bahá'i Publishing Trust, 1990 pocket-size edition, CXXII: p.260
p. 12.	Bahá'u'lláh, *Gleanings from the Writings of Bahá'u'lláh*, US Bahá'i Publishing Trust, 1990 pocket-size edition, XXVI: p.63
p. 13.	*ibid*, XCIV: pp.192-3
p. 14.	*ibid*, p.193
p. 15.	*ibid*, p.193-4
p. 16.	Bahá'u'lláh, *Tablets of Bahá'u'lláh revealed after the Kitáb-i-Aqdas*, 1988, pp.140-1
p. 17.	Bahá'u'lláh, *Gleanings from the Writings of Bahá'u'lláh*, US Baha'i Publishing Trust, 1990 pocket-size edition, LXXXV: p168
p. 18.	*ibid*, LXXIV: p142
p. 19.	*ibid*, LXXIV: p141-2
p. 20a	Bahá'u'lláh, *Tablets of Bahá'u'lláh revealed after the Kitáb-i-Aqdas*, 1988, pocket-size edition, p.168
p. 20b	Bahá'u'lláh, *The Promise of World Peace*. Universal House of Justice, Bahá'í World Centre, 1985, p.12
pp. 22-3.	'Abdu'l-Bahá, *Tablet to Auguste Forel*, George Ronald Publishers, 1978, pp.8-9
p. 24.	'Abdu'l-Bahá, *Tablets of 'Abdu'l-Bahá 'Abbas*, Bahá'í Publishing Committee, 1909, p. 178

p. 25.	Bahá'u'lláh, *Gleanings from the Writings of Bahá'u'lláh*, US Baha'i Publishing Trust, 1990, p.161-2
p. 27.	'Abdu'l-Bahá, *Tablets of 'Abdu'l-Bahá 'Abbas*, New York Bahá'í Publishing Committee, 1930, volume 1. p.205
p. 29a	'Abdu'l-Bahá, *The Promulgation of Universal Peace*, US Bahá'í Publishing Trust, 1982, p.226
p. 29b	'Abdu'l-Bahá, *Selections from the Writings of 'Abdu'l-Bahá*, Bahá'í World Centre, 1982, p.170-1
p. 30.	From a letter written on behalf of Shoghi Effendi to an individual believer, February 18th, 1954. *Lights of Guidance.* Bahá'í Publishing Trust, New Delhi, India, 1988. No. 391. p.115
p. 31.	Bahá'u'lláh, *Gleanings from the Writings of Bahá'u'lláh*, US Baha'i Publishing Trust, 1990 pocket-size edition, XCIII: p.186
p. 32.	First page of *Kitáb-i-Aqdas*, in Arabic, in the handwriting of 'Abdul'Bahá.
p. 33.	Bahá'u'lláh, *Tablets of Bahá'u'lláh revealed after the Kitáb-i-Aqdas*, 1988, pocket-size edition, pp.141-2
pp. 34-5.	'Abdu'l-Bahá, *Selections from the Writings of 'Abdu'l-Bahá*, Bahá'í World Centre, 1982, pp.41-2
pp. 36-7.	'Abdu'l-Bahá, *The Promulgation of Universal Peace*, US Bahá'í Publishing Trust, 1982, p.148
p. 38a	'Abdu'l-Bahá, *A Selection of Prayers.* US Bahá'í Publishing Trust, 1991, p.103
p. 38b	Adapted from Bahá'u'lláh, *Gems of Divine Mysteries,* Bahá'í World Centre, 2002, p.6
pp. 40-1.	*Selections from the Writings of 'Abdu'l-Bahá*, Bahá'í World Centre, 1982, p.36
p. 42.	Bahá'u'lláh, *The Hidden Words*, No. 19 from the Persian.
p. 44.	Bahá'u'lláh, *Tablets of Bahá'u'lláh revealed after the Kitáb-i-Aqdas*, 1988, p.143
p. 45.	Original revelation handwriting of Bahá'u'lláh

Visual imagery sampled from handwriting of Bahá'u'lláh and 'Abdu'l-Bahá and calligraphy of Mishkín-Qalam.

First Published in the UK in 2014 by
Intellect, The Mill, Parnall Road, Fishponds, Bristol, BS16 3JG, UK

First published in the USA in 2014
by Intellect, The University of Chicago Press, 1427 E. 60th Street, Chicago, IL 60637, USA

Copyright © 2014 Intellect Ltd

All rights reserved. No part of this publication may be reproduced, stored in a retrieval system, or transmitted, in any form or by any means, electronic, mechanical, photocopying, recording, or otherwise, without written permission.

A catalogue record for this book is available from the British Library.

Book Design: Corinne Randall
Publisher: Masoud Yazdani
ISBN: 978-1-78320-114-3
Printed and bound by Gomer Press Ltd.

Other books in the *Essential Insights* series.
Healing, Truthfulness, Mindfulness, Detachment, Openness, Oneness, Generosity, Gratefulness, Love, Simplicity, Transformation.